Contents

Front and Back Covers: Color illustrations courtesy of Wardley Products Company, Inc.; a neon tetra with neon tetra disease (front cover) and a characoid fish with bacterial infection (back cover). © 1979, Wardley Products Company, Inc.

Endpapers: Rainbow cichlids *(Herotilapia multispinosa),* photo by H.J. Richter (front endpaper) and marble hatchetfish *(Carnegiella strigata),* photo by Dr. H.R. Axelrod (back end paper).

Frontis: Anchor worms *(Lernaea cyprinacea)* with egg sacs, photo by W.A. Tomey.

For Marcus Kristopher

ISBN 0-87666-524-5

© 1979 by T.F.H. Publications, Inc.

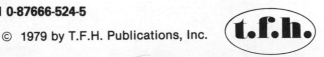

Distributed in the U.S. by T.F.H. Publications, Inc., 211 West Sylvania Avenue, PO Box 427, Neptune, NJ 07753; in England by T.F.H. (Gt. Britain) Ltd., 13 Nutley Lane, Reigate, Surrey; in Canada to the book store and library trade by Beaverbooks Ltd., 150 Lesmill Road, Don Mills, Ontario M38 2T5, Canada; in Canada to the pet trade by Rolf C. Hagen Ltd., 3225 Sartelon Street, Montreal 382, Quebec; in Southeast Asia by Y.W. Ong, 9 Lorong 36 Geylang, Singapore 14; in Australia and the South Pacific by Pet Imports Pty. Ltd., P.O. Box 149, Brookvale 2100, N.S.W. Australia; in South Africa by Valid Agencies, P.O. Box 51901, Randburg 2125 South Africa. Published by T.F.H. Publications, Inc., Ltd, the British Crown Colony of Hong Kong.

FISH DISEASES

DR. MARK DULIN

An anabantoid fish like *Osphronemus goramy* at left can survive without aeration in an aquarium because it has a special organ, called labyrinth, which enables it to utilize atmospheric oxygen. Photo by Dr. S. Frank. More typical fishes, such as the characoids and cichlids in this large tank, can not live very long without aeration. Public aquariums usually have generators which supply power during an emergency. Photo by Dr. H.R. Axelrod.

Health-Related Aspects of Keeping Fishes in Captivity

This book deals with the prevention, diagnosis and treatment of those diseases which most commonly affect tropical fishes maintained in captivity. By keeping fishes in an aquarium, you are subjecting them to an unnatural environment. In their natural habitat, tropical fishes are free to swim about, selectively eating those foods provided by nature. The accumulation of toxic metabolic waste byproducts does not become a threat to their health.

Non-polluted tropical streams are being aerated by nature. As natural waterways meander to the ocean, the water picks up atmospheric oxygen as it splashes and

tumbles over rocks and dams. Pond fishes receive supplemental oxygen during the day from aquatic vegetation. Still other tropical fishes have evolved to survive in waters with very low levels of dissolved oxygen. These labyrinth fishes, such as gouramis and bettas, have a specialized breathing structure which enables them to survive in warm, oxygen-deficient environments. Most tropical aquarium fishes are not this fortunate, however, and must rely on absorbing dissolved oxygen with their gills.

The fishes that you own have been deprived of their native habitat; they are no longer able to swim about and select natural foods. They are no longer exposed to nature's photoperiod of gradually increased light intensity which reaches a maximum and then slowly decreases toward darkness. In captivity, their instincts for survival are still keen, but their escape and avoidance reactions must be altered to their new, relatively small glass enclosure. It readily becomes apparent that the aquarist has assumed a high degree of responsibility for the health of fishes being maintained in captivity. If you are a conscientious aquarist, you will strive to provide your fishes with an optimum habitat for their survival. Of course, optimal conditions vary among species. It is beyond the scope of this book to list the optimal conditions for each of the species you might wish to keep in your aquarium. However, the main health-related factors which must be considered when keeping tropical fishes in captivity are listed below:

1. Nutrition
2. Selection of compatible species
3. Loading capacity of the aquarium
4. Heating
5. Aeration
6. Lighting
7. Filtration
8. pH control

NUTRITION

Unlike fishes in their natural environment, aquarium fishes are unable to selectively ingest natural foods. They must rely on their owners to provide them with a balanced diet. To ensure adequate nutrition, feeding a variety of both natural and processed foods is the best policy. Natural foods, both live and frozen, are the best insurance against vitamin deficiencies in your captive fishes. Most pet shops have an excellent assortment of both natural and processed foods.

SELECTION OF COMPATIBLE SPECIES

One of the most important considerations to remember when setting up an aquarium is species compatibility. It is not uncommon for beginning aquarists to stock the aquarium with fishes that are in no way compatible. Sometimes this results in an outright attack by the aggressor, with subsequent trauma to the fish under attack. At other times the outcome of harassment is more subtle; the fish under attack is stressed, may stop eating and becomes highly susceptible to infectious diseases. Each day you should observe your fishes for signs of aggression. Incompatible species must not be maintained in the same aquarium.

LOADING CAPACITY OF THE AQUARIUM

There is an overwhelming tendency to put too many fishes into a given aquarium. As a fish grows, so does its oxygen demands. Also, as a fish becomes larger, it excretes more metabolic wastes. Overcrowding can lead to anoxia (absence of oxygen) and the accumulation of toxic levels of metabolic waste products. A biological filter, whether it be an undergravel, a box filter or both, can only break down a certain quantity of excreta per hour. If the tank is overcrowded, the excretion of wastes may exceed the biofilter's capacity to break down these harmful elements. Exceeding

1. In the tropics, where sunlight is intense, the algae in a pond can grow profusely. Most fishes, except those with auxiliary breathing organs, can suffocate at night when the algae reduce the oxygon content of the water and increase its carbon dioxide content. Photo by Dr. H.R. Axelrod. 2. Bettas, also called Siamese fighting fish, do not require aeration in an aquarium.

your tank's carrying capacity also facilitates the transfer of parasites from one fish to another and causes environmental stress.

HEATING

The optimum temperature range for most tropical fishes is 76° to 85° F. (24° to 29° C.). There are many reliable thermostatically controlled aquarium heaters on the market. As is the case with other pieces of aquarium equipment, small children should not be permitted to tamper with these devices. There are a variety of aquarium cabinets available which not only prevent unwanted access to the life-giving support systems but also can make the aquarium setup more attractive.

AERATION

A dissolved oxygen level of 6 to 8 parts per million (ppm) is desirable. This is best accomplished by using an airstone or diffuser which is adjusted to produce very tiny bubbles. Remember that increases in altitude and temperature diminish the oxygen-carrying capacity of the water. Also, because the air pump picks up room air to oxygenate the tank, the room air should be fresh and clean. If paint fumes and tobacco smoke are in the room, these fumes can be forced into solution and may have an adverse effect on the fish.

LIGHTING

Most tropical fishes do best with a 12-hour light/dark photoperiod. Too little light prevents normal feeding activity. Direct sunlight or excess illumination from special plant lights may result in unwanted algal blooms.

FILTRATION

Unless the water is completely or partially changed at frequent intervals, some form of filtration apparatus will be required. The function of a *mechanical filter* is to remove particulate matter such as food, feces and tank debris. If allowed to decompose, decaying material not only diminishes the oxygen level in the tank but also provides a favorable environment for excessive bacterial growth. Tank detritus can also lodge in the gill lamellae, thus inhibiting normal respiration.

A *biological filter*, whether it be undergravel, box or a separate canister, functions to break down metabolic waste products. The byproducts of this decomposition process (especially ammonia & nitrites) can accumulate to toxic levels unless beneficial flora or bacteria in the genera *Nitrobacter* and *Nitrosomonas* are present. New biological filters will of course be lacking these beneficial bacteria, thus new aquariums must be "seeded" with these bacteria to ensure adequate biological breakdown from the time the fishes are first placed in the aquarium. During this two-week "breaking-in" procedure, the tank should be aerated and heated just as if fish were present. One method of seeding the aquarium is to mix a cup or two of gravel from an established filter with the gravel in your new filtration apparatus. Various "food" sources for these bacteria have been suggested (decaying raw clams or fish, decaying flake food, etc.). Regardless of what techniques you use to seed your new aquarium with beneficial bacteria, there is one important consideration to remember. Just as beneficial flora can be transferred from tank to tank, so can unwanted infectious agents, so be sure the tank donating gravel is free of infectious agents; from this time onward, before placing anything in your aquarium consider its potential to transmit disease. Also, don't forget that the beneficial flora is vital to the health of all fishes maintained in a closed-system. It should be protected from exposure to harmful antibiotics and therapeutics. Although not all medications have an adverse effect on this flora, some commonly used therapeutics (such as methylene blue and erythromycin) have been shown to kill these bacteria, thus stopping the nitrification process.

1

2

3

1. Plants increase faster than fish in a tank, so they should be reduced periodically. Photo by Dr. H.R. Axelrod. 2. Basic equipment for setting up a freshwater fish aquarium. Plastic plants are not toxic, and many of them are quite colorful. 3. A swordtail *(Xiphophorus helleri)* with exophthalmos, or popeye. A Frickhinger photo. 4. Deficiency of vitamin C can cause skeletal abnormalities which result in misshapen backs. Photo by Dr. Fred Meyer.

4

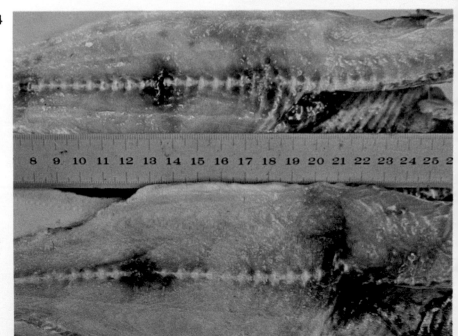

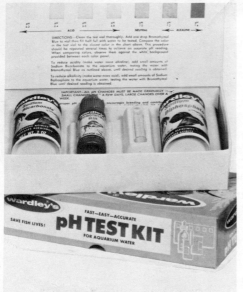

1

1. A pH kit will enable you to keep the water in your aquarium close to the type the fish requires. 2 and 3. A thermometer and a heater are important, because a reliable temperature control is an important part of the treatment of certain fish diseases.

2

3

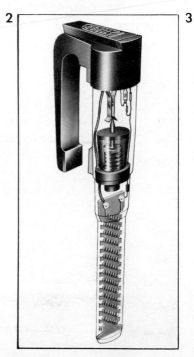

In addition to mechanical and biological filtration, many aquarists use *chemical filtration* to enhance the clarity of the tank and to absorb dissolved chemicals and gases which may be toxic to fishes. Activated charcoal is most commonly used to absorb various chemicals. If activated charcoal is used it should be well washed and aged in water prior to use. Also, just as activated charcoal binds with unwanted chemicals, it can also bind with therapeutic agents which you might eventually need to place in the aquarium. With some diseases, effective eradication is best accomplished by placing drugs in the aquarium. Should this be the only way to effectively control the disease, the activated charcoal will need to be removed during the treatment procedure.

pH CONTROL

Most aquarists are aware that pH is an important water quality factor which must be maintained within a relatively narrow range to ensure the well-being of your fishes. A variety of inexpensive and fairly accurate pH test kits are available at most pet stores. I will discuss why pH is important and what can be done to treat and avoid dangerous pH levels when I discuss acidosis and alkalosis in a later chapter. For now, I just want to make you aware of this concept and emphasize the need for monitoring the pH as one of the health-related factors which must be considered whenever tropical fishes are kept in captivity.

1. Guppies *(Poecilia reticulata)* with curvature of the spine caused by tuberculosis. Guppies can also suffer from a spinal deformity that is genetic, called hereditary lordosis. 2. A tetra with signs of bacterial infection: red spots, ragged fins. Illustration © 1979 by Wardley Products Co., Inc. 3. Bacteria can be identified by their affinity to dyes; the blue rod-shaped bacteria are harmless, while the reddish clumps of bacteria are pathogenic. Photo courtesy of Piscisan Ltd. 4. When subjected to certain chemicals, *Aeromonas* become fluorescent and visible for photography. Photo by D.H. Lewis.

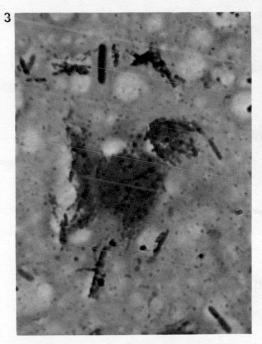

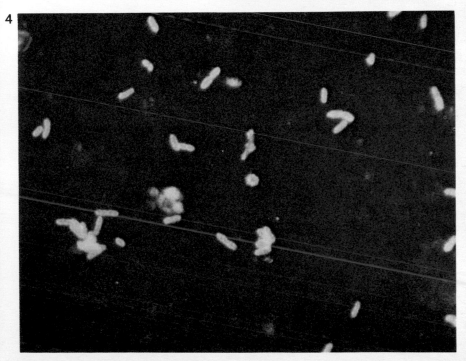

The tail-less condition of this cichlid, *Thysia ansorgii,* is congenital, not due to an accident or a disease. Photo by R. Zukal. *Below:* Natural mass fish deaths occur when the water is depleted of its oxygen supply; depletion can occur biologically (algal blooms), chemically (substances react with the oxygen), and physically (aeration barriers like oil slicks, etc.)

Non-Infectious Diseases

GASPING SYNDROME (ANOXIA)

Just like any other animal, fishes need a constant supply of oxygen to survive. Because oxygen is relatively scarce in water (0 to 14 ppm) as compared to air (260 ppm) and because water is about 800 times more dense than air, fishes must expend considerable amounts of energy to breathe. They must move large quantities of water past the respiratory exchange surfaces (gills) in order for adequate levels of dissolved oxygen to be transferred to the red blood cells for distribution to the rest of the body.

1

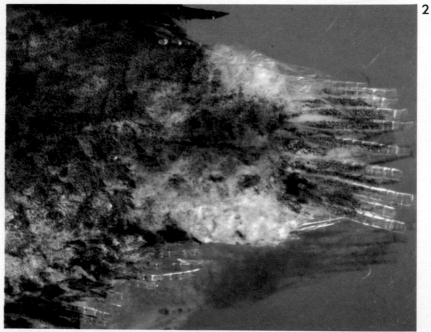

2

1. A spotted headstander *(Chilodus punctatus)* with tail rot. Illustration © 1979 by Wardley Products Co. 2. Advanced bacterial tail rot in a cichlid. 3. Lymphocystis disease in the tail of a green terror *(Aequidens rivulatus)*. 4. A discus fish *(Symphysodon aequifasciata)* with fungus growing on several areas of the body. Illustration © 1979 by Wardley Products Co.

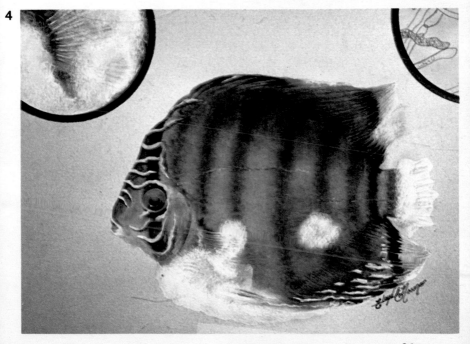

The dissolved oxygen level which should be maintained in the aquarium varies according to the species. Some fishes, such as the gouramis and bettas, can survive in oxygen-deficient water, but most fishes need a dissolved oxygen level of around 7-8 ppm. The warmer the water temperature, the less oxygen retention capacity of the water. With the warm water temperatures in tropical aquariums, aeration devices are required to ensure adequate levels of dissolved oxygen.

Fishes suffering from anoxia (lack of oxygen) will sustain tissue damage or die unless the dissolved oxygen level is quickly increased. Fishes suffering from hypoxia (insufficient oxygen reaching the tissues) are physiologically stressed. Clinical signs of a hypoxic condition include rapid shallow respiration with the opercles flared and the gills exposed. As the condition worsens these fish may begin to jump, swim irregularly or gasp for air at the surface of the aquarium. Upon exhaustion they become listless and may die with the opercles flared, mouth agape and gills very pale in color. If most of the fishes in the tank exhibit signs of respiratory distress, the dissolved oxygen level must be promptly restored or fish may begin to die within minutes. If the air pump is not working, a prompt water change may be the answer if suitable water is available. Once you have handled this acute emergency, try to figure out what caused the insufficient dissolved oxygen level. If the pump broke, your diagnosis may be obvious. Just remember that overcrowding, excessive temperatures, algal blooms and decaying organic matter can also lead to oxygen-deficient water.

POISONING

There are many ways in which aquarium fishes can become poisoned. One common way poisons enter the aquarium is via the air pump. Cigarette smoke, paint fumes and volatile insecticides are just some of the noxious substances which could be picked up by the air pump and forced into solution. Depending upon the nature of the poisonous substance, signs of poisoning may appear quickly after the substance is introduced or the signs may be slow to develop and the disease is said to have a chronic course.

Some aquarium fishes have been known to be poisoned by more direct means than by pumping air-borne substances into solution. Whether the offender is a young child with no ill intentions or a "mature" individual with destructive tendencies, poisonous substances are occasionally introduced directly into the aquarium by man. There have been numerous instances of bar room aquariums being dosed with alcoholic substances, possibly so a drunken humanoid could see if, like himself, fish can become drunk. Unfortunately, alcohol is a poison to fish, just as it is for man should sufficient quantities be administered too abruptly. Let us hope that your cocktail party guests are more considerate!

Sometimes an aquarist with the best intentions is directly responsible for poisoning his own fishes. The use of plastic buckets for water changes has been responsible for numerous fish mortalities. There is nothing wrong with using plastic buckets to transfer water to an aquarium *if* the bucket has never been previously used for cleaning or disinfecting around the house. Even well rinsed buckets can still contain lethal amounts of chlorine, Lysol or other commonly used household chemicals. Plastic buckets in particular seem to have an affinity for retaining residual amounts of various chemicals. If you use a plastic bucket for transferring water, make it "FOR AQUARIUM USE ONLY" and make certain it's never used for any other purpose.

Another method by which poisons can be introduced into the aquarium is by the direct transfer of certain algae into the aquarium. Although most algae are not harmful and may even be desirable in the balanced aquarium system, some species of algae are capable of producing ichthyotoxins. The aquarist should always be cautious of this when transferring food items or plants from native waters.

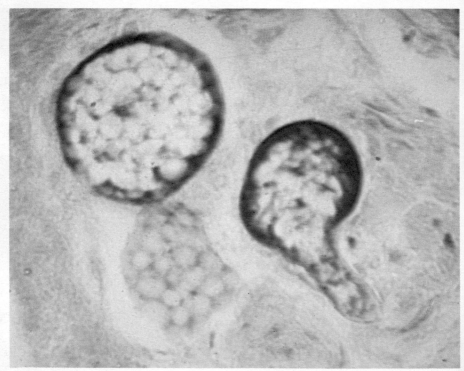

1. The kidney (at the top of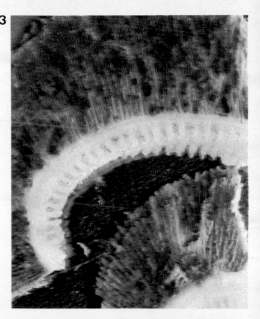
the body cavity) of a trout
with *Ichthyophonus*
disease. Photo by Dr. P.
Ghittino. 2. Enlarged photo
of the cysts of
Ichthyophonus in the
tissues of the kidney.
Some of the spores are in
the process of emerging.
Photo by Dr. H.-H.
Reichenbach-Klinke.
3. Branchiomycosis of the
gills of a carp. Photo by Dr.
P. Kinkelin. 4. Close-up of
Branchiomyces, the
causative agent of gill rot,
or branchiomycosis. Photo
by Dr. H.-H. Reichenbach-
Klinke.

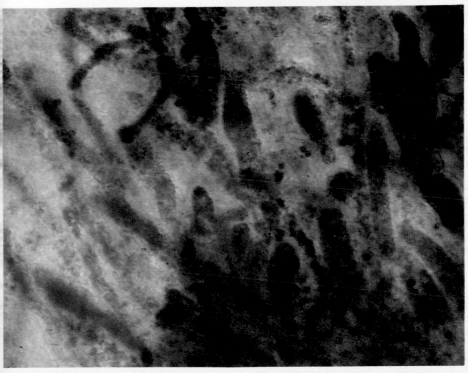

The last method of poisoning I would like to discuss is perhaps the most common. This is poisoning via the toxic excretions of the fishes themselves. Just as a man would die if waste products were not eliminated from his body, so fish also die if waste products are not eliminated from the aquarium. Actually, what we are talking about is fish-induced water pollution. Either because too many animals (remember that snails and newts eliminate wastes too!) are maintained in too small a tank or because the biological filtration system is not functioning properly, wastes have accumulated.

When excessive food and feces are allowed to decompose in the tank, they not only utilize precious oxygen but also release toxic waste materials. Fish eliminate nitrogenous wastes both with the urine and from the gills. Higher levels of ammonia are released from the gills during feeding, digestion, or periods of stress. Therefore, the ammonia-nitrogen level in the aquarium fluctuates depending on the amount of activity in the tank. A properly working biological filtration system can break down these poisonous elements into harmless elements providing the system is not overloaded.

Remember that the biological filtration system is dependent upon certain beneficial bacteria which utilize these wastes as an energy source. If these bacteria are destroyed (via certain antibacterials such as erythromycin or methylene blue) then the biological filter can no longer function properly. If the beneficial bacterial flora is destroyed, the aquarist faces the same problem as if he had never seeded the gravel with desirable bacteria in the first place (at least two weeks are required for the flora in a new bio-filter to become established).

Nitrite poisoning can be avoided if the aquarist seeds the tank with gravel from an established disease-free aquarium, avoids overcrowding, keeps the tank free of debris and protects the beneficial flora from antibacterial solutions.

28

Regardless of the cause of poisoning, corrective action is necessary if the fishes are to return to a state of health. In the case of an acute emergency, a prompt water change may be all that is required to save the fishes. At other times the poison-producing substance (certain algae for example) is more difficult to eliminate from the aquarium. The methods of treatment depend on the particular substance causing the poisoning. The real detective work in determining the cause of poisoning lies in your own hands. Once a cause-and-effect relationship has been established, you are on the way to correcting the situation. The important thing to remember is that the aquarium is a highly artificial environment. A delicate balance must be maintained and cautiously protected from the inadvertent administration of poisonous substances.

AGGRESSION

With experience, aquarists learn generalizations concerning the compatibility of certain species. Even the beginning aquarist soon finds out that certain species should not be placed in the same aquarium with more aggressive fishes. Sometimes the more aggressive fishes will attack subordinate fishes outright; other times the damage is more subtle. It has long been known that humans living under the strain of incompatibility are more prone to acquiring both infectious and noninfectious diseases. Likewise, animals maintained under stressful conditions are quite prone to acquiring disease. It makes little difference whether we are speaking of experimental monkeys with electrodes implanted in the brain, laboratory mice living with fear of being shocked by a student of experimental psychology or fishes being kept in close proximity with natural enemies—animals (including man) cannot be expected to remain healthy when living under adverse environmental conditions. The important concept to remember is that stress predisposes animals to acquiring diseases.

3

1. A goldfish *(Carassius auratus)* with lesions caused by *Saprolegnia*. 2. Enlarged photograph of the filaments of *Saprolegnia*. Photo courtesy of the U.S. Fish and Wildlife Service. 3. Fungusing eggs of a catfish *(Corydoras paleatus)*. Affected eggs must be removed to prevent the contamination of other eggs. Photo by H.J. Richter. 4. An archer fish *(Toxotes)* with a heavy fungal infection, which could be *Saprolegnia*. Frickhinger photo.

4

When stocking an aquarium, the beginning aquarist should talk with experienced hobbyists and ask reliable pet shop employees for advice. It is beyond the scope of this book to elaborate on species compatibility; many excellent books are available on this particular subject. As a point of illustration, let us examine why angelfish and tiger barbs are considered incompatible. Angelfish are territorial, aggressive and relatively inactive swimmers. Tiger barbs, on the other hand, are a schooling fish that are always on the move and prowling about for food. When a young tiger barb bites at the worm-like filamentous fins of a mature angelfish, you can expect some degree of retaliation on the part of the angelfish. Even if incompatible species learn to "cope" with one another, they still may be chronically stressed. Through understanding the fish's natural habitat and modes of existence, the aquarist can more readily come to appreciate its needs. When maintaining fishes in captivity, the needs for a pleasant and relaxed atmosphere must be met or you are failing to provide your fishes with an optimum environment.

Whenever adding new species to an established aquarium, realize that you may be playing havoc with the pecking order. A whole new set of territorial boundaries may need to be established before the newcomer finds its place in the social order. Sometimes rearranging aquarium decorations to subject both old and new fishes to a change of scenery will make the newcomers ascent into the social order more equitable. Regardless of how you go about adding a new fish to your tank, make sure you watch the fishes closely for signs of incompatibility. If you see aggressive behavior, remove the newcomer and place it in another aquarium.

MALNUTRITION
Dominance and competition are also important factors when we consider nutrition. Naturally the more aggressive

and larger fishes will out-compete the smaller or more inhibited fishes. It's up to the aquarist to see each gets its fair share.

The amount of diversification among fishes is almost incredible. Certainly these evolutionary changes favored survival in the wild or they would not have developed. One form of diversification is seen in the particular eating habits of a given species. There are carnivorous, herbivorous, and omnivorous fishes; there are fishes which filter plankton with their gill rakers, fishes that feed on detritus, and fishes which are voracious predators. There are benthic feeders, pelagic feeders and fishes which have evolved to feed directly from the water surface—even fishes which have evolved to "squirt down" prey that flies above the water surface.

Knowledge of your fishes' eating habits is important so you can offer your fishes the types of foods they like and present the food in such a manner that it is readily acceptable. Failure to provide your fishes with an adequate diet results in malnutrition. Even if only one essential amino acid is lacking the fish may become malnourished. The dietary formulation must be balanced and complete with all the necessary vitamins and minerals. Because your fishes can no longer roam about selectively feeding on those items they instinctively crave, it is up to you to provide them with a balanced diet.

It is doubtful that any single commercially prepared food is capable of providing all your tropical fishes with 100% adequate nutrition. Some vitamins are quite unstable, and it is therefore unlikely that a dried flake food is capable of containing proper vitamin levels, especially if that food has been on the shelf for any period of time. Certainly flake foods can provide many desirable nutrients, but to play it safe other types of foods should also be fed to your fishes.

Natural foods such as living, fresh or frozen plant and animal tissues are excellent sources of nutrients. Pet shops

1. Knowing the hardness of your water is important; unfavorable hardness factors can subject a fish to great stress—even death can result. 2. Commercially prepared fish foods are safe and nutritious. The risk of introducing pathogens into the tank is also minimal. 3. Remedies for the more common fish diseases are available in pet shops. 4. Inexpensive but reliable vibrator-type air pumps are handy for providing aeration/filtration in hospital tanks and small aquaria.

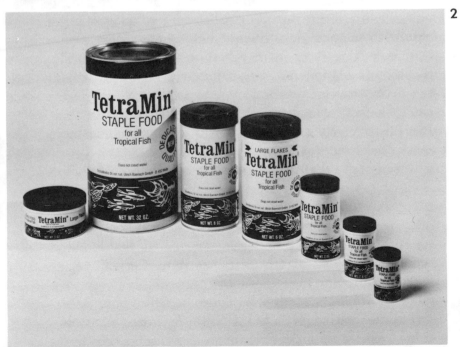

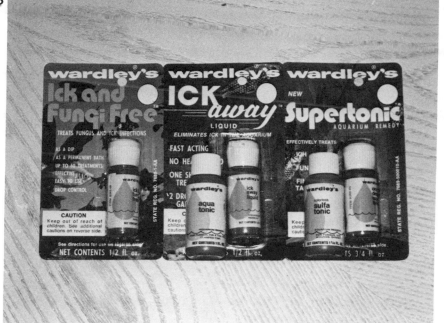

3

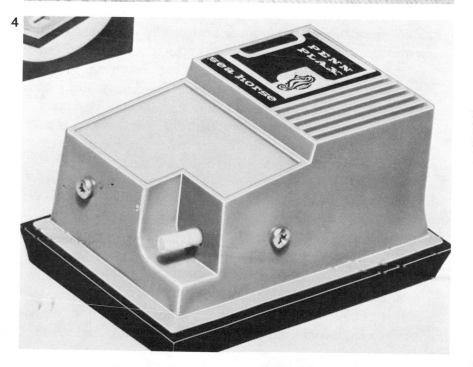

4

generally sell a wide variety of frozen foods. Live foods are often the most desirable source of food for fishes as long as pathogenic organisms are not introduced by these foods. Many of the "wild" foods are intermediate hosts for a variety of fish parasites such as roundworms and tapeworms. Cultured living animals are to be preferred over animals which have been captured in the wild.

Malnourished fishes have weakened body defenses and make easy prey for opportunistic pathogens which may already be present in the aquarium or may be lying dormant within various fish tissues, awaiting a chance to multiply and destroy vital organs. Feeding quality foods is both the treatment for malnutrition and the method by which malnutrition can be avoided.

ACIDOSIS, ALKALOSIS AND pH

Ever hear of the term pH? Sure you have! In this day of non-alkaline shampoos, I doubt if anyone has escaped the news media's explanation of the reasons for using non-alkaline shampoos and lotions. Technically speaking, pH is a measure of acidity or alkalinity expressed as the logarithm of the reciprocal of the hydrogen ion concentration. Sound confusing? Well, you need not be confused—just think of the pH scale as going from 0 to 14, with 0 being extremely acid and 14 being extremely alkaline. Neutral would then be at a pH of 7.0. Most freshwater fishes survive in waters with a pH ranging from 6.5 to 8.0; however, each species has a pH preference. Some fishes which originate in tropical bog waters rich in humic acid actually prefer acid waters in the neighborhood of 5.5. Many tetras and the discus are examples of such "acid loving" fishes. Some killifishes and the Rift Lake cichlids, on the other hand, seem to have a preference for alkaline waters with a pH of around 8.5.

It is impossible to provide each species with its optimum pH in a large community tank—in these instances a neutral pH is probably best. The aquarist should become knowledgeable about the particular species being kept in captivity. This includes finding the fish's temperature and pH preference. Many fishes will not spawn or perform optimally unless you satisfy their specific water quality requirements, pH included.

BUFFERING CAPACITY OF WATER

Perhaps more important than the pH is the actual buffering capability of the water. Technically speaking, a buffer is any substance in a fluid which tends to lessen the change in hydrogen ion concentration which otherwise would be produced by adding acids or alkalis. You are probably wondering why you need to be concerned with buffers since you won't be adding either acids or alkalis to your aquarium. The reason is because the fishes and plants excrete compounds which need to be buffered. In poorly buffered water, fish respiration alone can substantially lower the pH and lead to acidosis. Also, in poorly buffered water the photosynthetic action of plants can deplete the water of free carbon dioxide, thereby raising the pH and causing alkalosis. This is especially true during the day, when plants take in CO_2 and give off oxygen. The most common carbonates which act as buffer reserves in water are those of calcium and magnesium. With this reserve present, plants can still obtain the necessary carbon dioxide from the dissolved calcium or magnesium carbonate. Without this reserve they can only obtain the free carbon dioxide derived from plant and fish respiration. Once the free carbon dioxide is gone, alkalosis can result. Remember that at night this process is reversed and the plants take in oxygen and give off carbon dioxide. This is why waters with aquatic vegetation generally have a lower pH in the morning than they do in the evening.

You really don't have to thoroughly understand this process (biogenous calcification and decalcification) to be a successful aquarist. Just remember that within your aquarium there is a biological balance which is continually fluctuating. In no way does your aquarium have a biological equilibrium such as you would expect to find in a pond. Your aquarium is a highly artificial environment, and artificial influences such as the use of proper substrate, temperature, lighting and filtration are necessary to keep the water quality in a normal range. Unless you enjoy tinkering with water chemistries and adding carbonates for their buffering effect, just use suitable water for rearing fish, avoid excessive plant growth and give the tank frequent water changes with suitable water.

ACIDOSIS

Various species of fishes have different pH preferences. When the pH is maintained below their acceptable range, acidosis can result. Fishes suffering from acidosis act "hyper." These jittery fishes make rapid movements and have a tendency to jump out of the water. The acid water damages the gills so these fishes may show signs of respiratory distress such as rapid breathing and gasping at the surface. The skin and fins may also become damaged as evidenced by reddening of the skin and fraying of the fins.

The principal cause of acidosis is too many fishes in water which is too soft. There are no buffers to handle the carbon dioxide which they produce, and excess carbon dioxide lowers the pH into the acidic range. To handle the emergency at hand you could either make a water change with suitable water or add sodium bicarbonate (baking soda) or dibasic sodium phosphate for its buffering effect. To prevent recurrences make certain the water has a reserve buffering system composed of various carbonates (use hard water), and don't overload the tank with too many animals (frogs and snails also give off carbon dioxide!).

ALKALOSIS

Some waters are highly alkaline because of natural causes

such as leaching of minerals from the soil. Using water which is slightly on the alkaline side of neutrality is generally quite acceptable for fishes in a mixed community tank; however, if the tank becomes increasingly more alkaline, it can become unsuitable. Again, it is the buffers which are responsible for keeping the pH from becoming too alkaline. Calcium and magnesium carbonates in water will absorb excessive acids until they themselves are used up. If the buffer reserve is depleted, alkalosis can result. The main cause of buffer depletion and hence alkalosis stems from excessive plant growth. Algal blooms and growing plants may consume all the free carbon dioxide, thereby forcing the pH into an undesirable alkaline range.

Fishes suffering from alkalosis generally exhibit signs of distress which are similar to those seen in acidosis. Erosion of the gills, fraying of the fins and development of a milky turbidity on the skin are typical manifestations of this disease. To confirm that the fishes are indeed suffering from alkalosis, the pH of the water should be checked.

Replacing the water with suitable water or adding buffering agents such as monobasic sodium phosphate will correct the immediate problem, but corrective action must be taken to prevent future reoccurrences. I'm not one to recommend plastic plants, but if you can't curtail the growth of plants that may be your best bet. If you must keep your tank decorated with aquatic vegetation, make sure the water is not too soft and don't expose the tank to direct sunlight. Excessive plant growth in water which is too soft is not the only cause of alkalosis; the use of coral in freshwater tanks can also make the water too alkaline.

GAS BUBBLE DISEASE

Although gas bubble disease is occasionally encountered in coldwater aquariums and at fish hatcheries, it seldom causes problems in household aquariums. It does warrant some attention, however, because aquarists may confuse

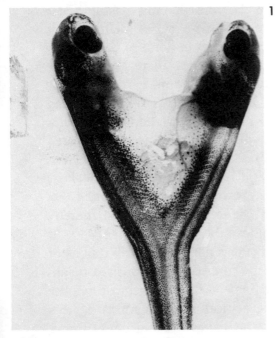

Non-infectious abnormalities in fish:
1. Siamese twins resulting from abnormal cleavage (cell division) of the egg. Photo by Dr. H.-H. Reichenbach-Klinke. 2. Dorsal hump due to old age in a swordtail (*Xiphophorus helleri*). Photo by R. Zukal. 3. Curvature of the spine in guppies, possibly a genetic defect due to inbreeding. However, the condition can be produced by infectious disease, too. Photo courtesy of New York Zoological Society. 4. Egg binding (inability to lay eggs) in *Garra taeniata*. Photo by R. Zukal.

bubbles adhering to the surface of a fish with this disease. For gas bubble disease to occur, the bubbles must be *within* the fish, not on the surface of the fish.

If cooler water is added to the tank, bubbles will form as the solution warms and may adhere to the mucous layer of the fish's skin. You can readily observe this phenomenon by filling a glass with cold tap water and allowing it to warm to room temperature. Cold water holds more gas than warm water; consequently, as the water warms, bubbles will appear and then leave the solution.

It is quite difficult to force enough gas into solution in a warmwater aquarium to produce clinical signs of gas bubble disease—but it can be done. In fish hatcheries or public aquariums where large power filter pumps are used, air leaks can develop on the intake side of the pump. This air, when sucked in through a loose connection or faulty seal, can produce a supersaturated condition of both oxygen and nitrogen.

Another method of supersaturating the water with atmospheric gases is to place new, unwashed carbon in a sealed canister. Since the carbon has not been presaturated with water, air in the activated carbon can be forced into the water when the system is turned on after cleaning.

Although rare, another way in which the aquarium can become dangerously supersaturated with gas is via an extreme amount of plant photosynthesis. During periods of intense light radiation and a calm air/water interface, plants and algae have been known to supersaturate the aquarium with oxygen and cause clinical signs of gas bubble disease.

Gas bubble disease has been likened to the "bends" which scuba divers experience when they surface too quickly without decompression stops or to aviators' decompression sickness. One fundamental difference between the condition in man *vs.* fish is that in fish a sudden reduction in external pressure is not required in order for bubbles to form. These tiny air bubbles enter the capillary beds and may coalesce to form large bubbles which can lodge in major vessels. When these air emboli block circulation to vital organs, death can occur.

If the water is mildly supersaturated or if the fish species is somewhat resistant to the effects of gas bubble disease, death may not occur; however, clinical signs of disease may be observed. In these mildly affected fish the tips of the fins may become white due to blockage of the small capillaries which supply blood to this area. When affected fish are held up to a light source, bubbles are most readily detected between the fin rays but may also be noticed within any of the external body surfaces including inside the mouth and below the surface of the eye. Small fishes and newly hatched fry show signs of abnormal buoyancy; these fishes may swim belly-up or in an erratic manner near the surface. Because of the subcutaneous air, moribund fishes are seen floating rather than sinking.

Gas bubble disease can be avoided by not using powerful biological filtration pumps or by making sure these pumps are operating effectively and the seals and fittings are airtight. Also avoid an overabundance of plant photosynthesis and follow the directions when adding new charcoal to the filter. Always prewash the charcoal and allow it to become saturated with water—especially before placing it into a sealed canister.

Should a case of gas bubble disease occur, there are ways to reduce the severity of the problem. If the fishes are affected only slightly, repair or removal of the faulty pump plus vigorous agitation of the water may be all that is required. Severely affected fishes will probably not survive. Several atmospheres of pressure would be required to decompress a fish, and it requires a very sturdy container to tolerate this type of air pressure. If such a container is available, this treatment would help force the gas emboli out of the fish's body.

DEVELOPMENTAL ABNORMALITIES

Abnormalities in a fish's anatomy or coloration can result from either hereditary defects or from abnormal individual development (defects acquired after birth). A variety of adverse physical and chemical conditions as well as infectious diseases are capable of inducing hereditary deformities. Trauma, malnutrition and various infectious agents are capable of causing ontogenetic abnormalities (defects acquired after birth).

Hereditary defects result when mutations occur in the genetic make up. Mutations are sudden, heritable changes in the structure of the genetic material; these mutations constitute the principal raw material with which nature works to bring about evolution. If these evolutionary changes favor survival, these new strains are considered successful; however, if these mutations in genetic material lead to an adverse effect on the continued survival of the species, they are considered unsuccessful variants doomed to extinction.

Over thousands of years, fishes have become modified in such a way that the chances of survival in the wild are increased. These evolutionary trends toward specialization have led to less intra-species competition for food, shelter and breeding grounds and more successful defense mechanisms. If a mutant developed which could not successfully compete against another species, it died and the gene pool it carried was lost. For example, if a mutant developed which stood out like a sore thumb (such as an albino), it was probably eaten by predators. If it did survive to maturity, it was likely sterile or incapable of attracting a mate for the spawning ritual.

Records of fish culture among Egyptians, Romans, Chinese and various Indo-Pacific peoples date back for centuries. By cultivating fishes in an artificial environment, strains which would never be successful in the wild have become firmly established in artificial habitats. Consider

Some mutations that are highly prized by goldfish fanciers (such as the bubble-eye goldfish shown here) can survive only in captivity. Such fishes can not compete with a normal fish in the wild.

man's interference as bastardizing the gene pool if you will, but many of these man-caused mutant strains have become some of the aquarist's most prized possessions. Several thousand dollars have been paid for individual koi, colorful Japanese mutations of ordinary carp.

Of course not all mutations are desirable. These undesirable offspring are considered to have developmental abnormalities. One congenital deformity which is not unusual among inbred fishes is a two-headed or "Siamese" twin condition. Torsion of the swim bladder resulting in the fish swimming on its side is another common developmental anomaly. Defects not only cause undesirable changes in the skin color, bones, fins and scales, but they have also caused various organs to develop abnormally so that affected fishes may be sterile, die of organ dysfunction or perhaps exhibit bizarre behavior.

45

Closeup of the head and forebody of a fish infected with ich. The fish seems sprinkled with salt; each spot is a capsule containing developing parasites. Photo by G.L. Timmerman. *Below:* Spores of *Myxosoma cerebralis,* the cause of the dreaded whirling disease of trout. It affects all ages, and survivors are generally deformed. Photo by Dr. P. Ghittino.

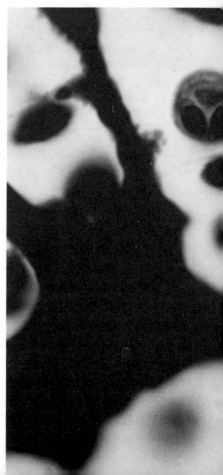

Infectious Diseases

BACTERIAL DISEASES

There are many bacterial diseases of fish. Like it or not, bacteria capable of harming your fish can gain entrance into your aquarium. Many of these harmful bacteria can be kept out of your aquarium by providing your fishes with an optimum habitat, but occasionally pathogenic bacteria may gain entrance into the aquarium through no fault of the aquarist. For example, a newly acquired specimen may appear perfectly healthy throughout the two-week quarantine yet be harboring large numbers of virulent bacteria. Such a fish is an *asymptomatic carrier*; that is, the fish is infected with the bacteria but shows no evidence of being diseased.

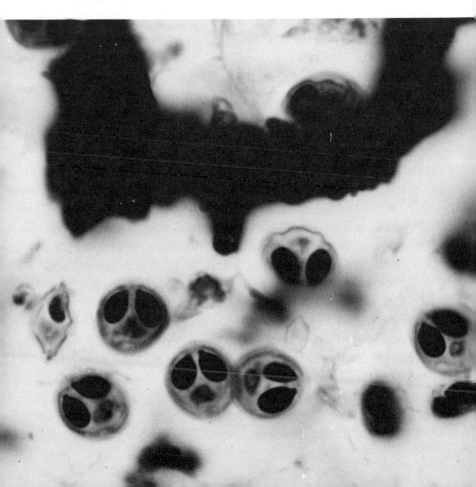

It undoubtedly suffered from the bacterial disease at one time, then recovered and became immune. Although immune, these asymptomatic carriers can harbor infective organisms and shed them in the feces. Asymptomatic carriers of disease occur throughout the animal kingdom, man included. It is beyond the scope of this book to discuss many of the other ways pathogenic bacteria can enter your aquarium. Suffice it to say that harmful bacteria can—and undoubtedly will—someday enter your aquarium.

Now, just because these bacteria are there does not automatically mean your fishes will all become diseased. If your fishes are healthy and maintained in a clean aquarium with the various water chemistry parameters (temperature, pH, dissolved oxygen, etc.) maintained within the optimal range, then your bacterial disease problems will likely be minimal.

However, if your fishes are suffering from malnutrition, previous injury (such as attacks from more aggressive fishes) or are environmentally stressed by adverse water chemistries, overcrowding, etc., then the chances of becoming infected are greatly increased. Remember, bacteria multiply quickly in dirty water, and water is an excellent vehicle for fish-to-fish transmission of bacteria. The higher the bacterial load in the water, the greater the chances of these organisms gaining entrance into your fishes. If the fishes are not in an optimal state of health, have no previous immunity to the particular bacteria and are exposed to more pathogenic bacteria than their body defenses can handle (critical mass), then they will become diseased.

The clinical signs of disease will vary according to the particular bacteria which has infected the fish. Some bacterial diseases have a short and relatively severe course and are referred to as *acute* bacterial diseases. Those bacterial diseases which persist over a long period of time are known as *chronic* bacterial diseases. When large numbers of fishes develop signs of disease almost simultaneously, then you are confronted with an epizootic. An epizootic caused by a highly virulent strain of bacteria is one of the most serious problems an aquarist can be faced with. How do you know when your fishes are affected with a bacterial disease and what can you do to treat these diseased fishes? Read on, as I will list some of the signs of common diseases and try to lead you down the path to a successful cure.

Some of the signs of an acute systemic bacterial disease include reddening at the base of the fins, around the vent, along the lateral line and of the mouth. Generally the fins become frayed and the eyes may appear clouded. These fish rapidly become listless, refuse to eat and may die if treatment is not initiated soon. These acute systemic bacterial diseases can be caused by any one of many species of bacteria. Members of the genera *Aeromonas* and *Pseudomonas* are often the ones responsible for these epizootics. Knowing the particular species of bacteria responsible for an acute bacterial disease is not really that important. What is important is being able to recognize that bacteria are responsible for the disease and providing the sick fish with an effective course of therapy. There are many antibacterial agents on the market, many of which are packaged for aquarium use. Some of these drugs are antibiotics (micro-organism-produced antimicrobial agents) while others, such as sulfa drugs, are classified as chemotherapeutics. Generally a 5- to 7-day course of therapy with a broad-spectrum antibiotic will cure the majority of acute bacterial diseases of fish. Unfortunately many aquarists have misused antibiotics in the past by using low, sub-therapeutic dosages. This has resulted in the evolution of many drug-resistant strains. Some of the antibacterials which have been overused and abused include the sulfas, penicillins and Tetracycline. Therefore, it is advisable to avoid the use of these drugs and use one of the newer broad-spectrum antibiotics such as Furanace. This antibiotic is readily available at most pet shops. When fish are placed in the proper dosage solution of Furanace (one 3.8 mg. capsule per 10 gallons of water), high antibiotic levels occur within the fish's circulatory system.

Other antibiotics which effectively control a wide variety of bacterial diseases include chloramphenicol, gentamicin and Kanamycin. When placed in solution, the dosage of *either* chloramphenicol, gentamicin or Kanamycin is 250 mg./5 gallons of water. The treatment should be conducted in a separate treatment tank containing adequately oxygenated water which is free of chlorine and has the same pH and temperature as the display tank. Diseased fish should be maintained in a therapeutic solution for 5- to 7-days even if the fish show signs of improvement during the first three days. To avoid the toxic accumulation of metabolic wastes and to maintain a therapeutic level of the drug, siphon out 25% of the water from the treatment tank every other day and refill with fresh, suitable water. After the water is replaced add an additional 200 mg. of the selected drug.

There are several reasons why I encourage aquarists to conduct antibacterial treatments in a separate bare all-glass aquarium and not in the exhibition tank. The main reason is that many antibiotics kill the beneficial bacterial flora in the tank. These "good guys" are needed in the gravel and biofilter to break down the fishes' metabolic wastes. Without this beneficial flora, toxic levels of ammonia and nitrite can accumulate. Furthermore, it is very difficult to calculate a therapeutic dosage of antibiotic when tank debris and activated charcoal are rapidly binding with the drug, thus rendering it ineffective. Don't place antibiotics in the exhibition tank, but instead remove the diseased fish and place them in a separate tank for treatment.

VIRAL DISEASES

Scientists have discovered several viral diseases of fishes, and many more will likely be discovered in the near future. It has been shown that fishes living in polluted waters have a much higher incidence of "cancer" than those same species which inhabit clean waters. One of the most common viral diseases of tropical fishes is lymphocystis. A contagious pox virus is responsible for this disease. Affected fishes develop wart-like lesions on the body surfaces. Some lesions may resemble cauliflower, while others are separate white to gray firm nodules. These lesions are most commonly seen on the fins and about the mouth.

Fish are presumably infected by ingesting lymphocystis cells that flake off the lesion or by actual nipping and picking at diseased fishes. It's also possible that the released viral particles invade the skin cells of other fishes, causing hypertrophy (enlargement) of the skin cells as the virus takes over the normal cell machinery.

Infected fishes should be quarantined for a minimum of two months while their immune response brings about a spontaneous cure. If lesions about the mouth become so severe as to interfere with eating, they can be surgically removed or treated with liquid nitrogen applications in the same manner in which human and animal warts are removed. There is no specific cure for viral diseases of fishes; however, research is under way to prevent these diseases by the use of immunizing agents (vaccines).

FUNGAL DISEASES

Fishes can be infected with both internal and external fungal diseases. The most common fungal diseases of tropical fishes include ichthyophonus disease (an internal fungal disease caused by *Ichthyophonus hoferi*); branchiomycosis or "fungal gill rot" (an acute fungal infection of the fish's gills caused by fungi in the genus *Branchiomyces*); and saprolegniasis (external fungal infections of the fish's skin and fins).

ICHTHYOPHONUS DISEASE

Ichthyophonus disease occurs in a wide variety of marine and freshwater fishes. This internal fungal invader may damage the heart, skeletal muscle, liver, kidney or brain. When the fungus invades the brain of aquarium fishes, clinical signs associated with an impaired central nervous system develop. They may appear listless and exhibit bizarre swimming behavior; exophthalmos (popeye) is also observed if the optic nerves are infected.

There is no known cure for ichthyophonus disease; generally by the time the fish shows signs of having the malady, the disease has progressed so far that treatments are futile. Fungizone (Amphotericin B) may prove worthwhile in treating valuable fishes; however, its effectiveness has not yet been demonstrated.

Fishes acquire this disease by eating infected tissues of other fishes and invertebrates (especially copepods). Upon ingestion the spores liberate amoeboid bodies which traverse the intestinal mucosa to reach the blood stream for systemic distribution, germination and spore production in new organs. Upon maturation spores are again released into the environment via excrement, lesions or the death and decay of the diseased host. Released spores have remained viable and infectious for several months.

To avoid introducing this disease into an aquarium, only quality aquarium foods or healthy fishes or invertebrates should be used for food. If an aquarium fish is suspected of having *Ichthyophonus* disease, it should be promptly removed from the exhibition tank.

BRANCHIOMYCOSIS

Branchiomycosis or "fungal gill rot" is an acute fungal infection of the fish's gills and is characterized by intravascular growth by members of the fungal genus *Branchiomyces*. Fishes affected with branchiomycosis exhibit signs of anoxia and loss of appetite. Hemorrhagic spots surrounded by whitened areas may occur on the gill lamellae. This fungal invader penetrates the lamellar vessels, causing enlargement and distortion of affected lamellae. Water rich in nutritive organic substances tends to favor the appearance of branchiomycosis; therefore overfeeding should be avoided as this adds to the buildup of organic wastes. There is no known cure for branchiomycosis.

SAPROLEGNIASIS (FUNGUS DISEASE)

The name saprolegniasis is commonly applied to any cotton-like growth of fungus on the fish's skin, gills or incubating eggs. Actually, *Saprolegnia* is not the only genus of fungus known to attack fishes, but it is by far the most common fungal invader of damaged tissues. These fungi are considered to be ubiquitous aquatic saprophytes which act only as opportunistic secondary invaders.

The most common clinical signs of saprolegniasis are patches of white to brownish cotton-like masses on the body surface, gills, eyes or fins. When viewed through the water surface, these tufts of hyphae resemble tufts of cotton wool—hence the name "cotton wool disease." The fungus penetrates the surface of the skin, fins or gills, giving rise to areas of necrosis (cell death). In the later stages of the disease, ulcerations occur, exposing the underlying musculature. In severe cases the entire body surface may be covered with the fungus prior to death.

Among egg-layers, there is the problem of fungi developing on the surface of incubating eggs. Initially the fungus attacks dead eggs; however, if these eggs are not removed, the fungus can spread to nearby living eggs, which suffocate in a mass of fungal hyphae.

Because most species of *Saprolegnia* are secondary opportunistic pathogens, trauma from excessive handling and otherwise damaging the skin or fin surfaces should be avoided. Dietary inadequacies can also predispose the fish to fungal attack. Aquarium fishes are more susceptible following attacks from more aggressive fishes or after receiving skin abrasions from sharp aquarium objects. Localized areas of saprolegniasis can be treated by swabbing the affected area with an antifungal agent such as 2% Mercurochrome or a malachite green solution (1:15,000). Furanace therapy is also often used in conjunction with the topical swabbing of the lesion.

As an aid in the control of fungus attack of incubating eggs, the dead eggs should be removed daily. Various methods of controlling egg fungus with chemical prophylaxis are also commonly employed. Methylene blue solutions have been extensively used for incubating eggs of tropical fishes. Suggested treatments for egg fungus include a one hour bath in either copper sulfate or malachite green solutions at the rate of 5 ppm or a 15-minute bath in a 1:500 formalin solution (2000 ppm). Treatments can be given on a daily basis until the fungus is controlled; however, treatments should not be given close to hatching time.

PROTOZOAN DISEASES

The single-celled protozoans are particularly prevalent in the aquatic environment, so it is not surprising that some of these organisms have become modified into fish parasites. Most of the aquatic protozoa are free-living, existing on bacteria and organic debris; however, some protozoa attach to fish for a free ride while feeding on particulate matter in the water. Still other protozoa have adapted to become obligate fish parasites, existing solely at the expense of the host. Protozoan parasites may exist not only on the skin and gills of fishes, but also within the blood stream, inside cells and within various tissues and organs.

Protozoan diseases of fishes are especially prevalent among captive fishes, for it is here that adverse environmental factors such as overcrowding, excessive accumulation of organic material and malnutrition are most likely to occur. Aquariums also provide a favorable environment for protozoan growth and transfer while all too often providing an unfavorable habitat for the development of fishes.

OODINOSIS

Oodinosis, commonly referred to as rust or velvet disease, affects a wide variety of freshwater aquarium fishes. The disease can have an explosive character, killing the fishes within a few days, or it can be so mild that affected fishes show no gross evidence of infection. Diseased fishes tend to lose their normal body color, and in advanced cases the skin may appear dark gray or yellowish, hence the term velvet disease.

Two species of *Oodinium* have been described as causing outbreaks of velvet disease among various species of freshwater aquarium fishes. *O. limneticum* attacks many species of tropical fishes, although it is of particular importance in the killifish, affecting both adults and newly hatched fry. *O. pillularis* has been reported in the gouramis, paradise fish, tetras, white cloud mountain minnows, platies, swordtails, rasboras and the barbs.

Tropical fishes affected with *Oodinium* exhibit a variety of clinical signs depending on the location and severity of the infection. When the gills are severely attacked, fishes exhibit signs of respiratory distress. Scratching the opercles on aquarium objects, rapid breathing and periods of rapid erratic swimming commonly occur. It is usually when the skin becomes infected that the aquarist recognizes a disease exists. The clinical signs of oodinosis may resemble "ich" (caused by the ciliated protozoan *Ichthyophthirius*), except the individual *Oodinium* parasites (recognizable with microscopic examination) are much smaller and have different morphological characteristics. Fishes affected with oodinosis develop a velvety or "dusty" appearance on the skin, oftentimes giving the fish a gold hue, while other times the skin is whitish and cloudy.

In advanced cases, the skin may even become dark gray and begin to peel away in strips. If the fish survives, secondary bacterial and fungal invasion commonly occurs following the initial skin damage. In cases of chronic oodinosis, deaths occur sporadically over the course of several weeks.

The best preventative measure for avoiding this disease is to quarantine all new specimens and closely observe them for two weeks prior to placing them in the exhibition tank. One common preventative treatment used by aquarists raising the annual killifish *Nothobranchius* is to add one teaspoon of aquarium salt per gallon of tank water. This procedure reduces the incidence of oodinosis among this salt-tolerant species, newly hatched fry included. Methylene blue and acriflavine also have been used prophylactically; however, the long term use of acriflavine has been shown to cause liver damage and sterility.

Copper sulfate treatment is probably the most effective treatment for external *oodinium* infections; the recommended therapeutic level of free copper ions is 0.15 ppm. This level should be maintained over a two-week period. Aquarium plants should be removed, disinfected, and maintained outside the display tank during copper therapy since this chemical is toxic to plants.

COSTIASIS

The external protozoan parasites in the genus *Costia* are among the most troublesome ectoparasites of tropical fishes. Like ich, *Costia* species are obligate parasites and therefore die unless they have access to a suitable host. These parasites attach to the host by means of a flat disc and feed by extending microtubules into the host cells. The irritation caused by attachment and feeding results in excessive mucus production which commonly causes a grayish white to bluish film on the fish's body. When the gills are heavily infected the fish may exhibit signs of respiratory distress. Heavily infected fish can also die.

Costiasis can easily be prevented in tropical aquarium fishes by keeping the water temperature above 29 °C.

(84 °F.). This temperature reduces the oxygen-carrying capacity of the water so supplemental oxygen is required for all but those specialized fishes which can survive in oxygen-deficient water.

Various commercial remedies are available to treat costiasis. One old standby remedy for stubborn cases is a 30-minute bath in a formalin solution (30 drops of formaldehyde per gallon of water).

"ICH"

"Ich" (pronounced ic*k*) is the most commonly diagnosed parasitic disease of freshwater tropical fishes. *Ichthyophthirius multifiliis,* the ciliated protozoan which causes this disease, is an obligate fish parasite; that is, the mature organism can survive only by feeding on the epithelial cells and tissue fluids of fishes. It cannot survive long periods of host deprivation.

If *Ichthyophthirius multifiliis* gains entrance into your aquarium, the "swarmer" stage will bore into the skin and gill cells of your fish, causing severe irritation. Affected fish may scratch the opercles on aquarium objects, have bizarre swimming behavior ("flashing"), show loss of appetite, become anemic (pale gills) and show signs of respiratory distress such as rapid breathing and gasping. Usually small white pustules are produced where the parasite is located; however, in some instances the diseased fish die before the characteristic white spots appear.

There are a wide variety of ich remedies on the market which will bring about a successful cure. In the case of labyrinth fishes such as gouramis and bettas, however, no drugs may be required to cure this disease. Apparently the organism cannot survive five successive days of 90 °F. (30 °C.) water temperatures, but neither can many fish! Thermo-therapy should only be used on these heat-resistant species. Stressing an already sick non-labyrinth fish by raising the temperature to this level is not advisable.

When using any commercial formulation, be sure to read the manufacturer's recommendations and remember that these chemicals have no effect on those parasites embedded in the skin. Because they only kill the free-swimming stages, therapeutic levels must be maintained for five to seven days.

CHILODONELLA

Like the protozoan parasite which causes "ich," *Chilodonella* is an obligate parasite of freshwater fishes. It cannot survive for very long without access to a fish host. *Chilodonella* is sometimes referred to as the "heart-shaped" parasite because it may have a slight indentation on the posterior end, giving it something of a heart-shape when examined microscopically. *Chilodonella* is primarily a parasite of debilitated fishes, although it can spread from these sick fishes to infect healthy fishes.

Chilodonella feeds upon the cells which cover th fishes' gills and body surfaces. Heavily infected fishes develop a gray to bluish white slimy covering on the skin. This coating is particularly noticeable on the head or on the body of darkly colored fishes. When this slime layer is examined microscopically, large numbers of the ciliated parasite can be observed. In the later stages of infection, strips of skin fall from the fish's body. When the gills are heavily attacked, the fish demonstrates erratic swimming behavior ("flashing") and may scrape against the sides and bottom.

Because *Chilodonella* generally only becomes a serious problem when fishes are stressed or debilitated, it is of utmost importance to keep your fishes in a good state of heaith. All new fishes should be quarantined and observed for signs of disease prior to placing them in an established aquarium.

Generally speaking, the same drugs which control "ich" are effective in destroying this parasite. Some of the chemicals which have been effective include: trypaflavine, acriflavine, aquarol, formalin, malachite green, methylene blue, salt and potassium permanganate.

TRICHODINA

Many species of trichodinids can cause serious harm to tropical aquarium fishes. The bodies of these protozoan parasites are circular when seen from below and hat-shaped when viewed from the side. They have circularly arranged rows of "teeth" which can severely damage the epithelial cells of both the fish's skin and gills.

Trichodina infections of the skin cause excessive mucus production and the formation of a bluish white film on the fish's body, similar to but usually less pronounced than that seen in costiasis. When the gills are heavily parasitized, the fishes show signs of being affected by a respiratory irritant. "Flashing" and scraping the opercles on aquarium objects are typical signs. Diseased fishes tend to be sluggish and show a disinterest in feeding. If left untreated, the fins of affected fishes become badly frayed, resulting in a tattered appearance. In some instances the parasite has been responsible for the complete erosion of gill filaments and subsequent death of the fish.

Fortunately, *trichodina* is one of the easier protozoan parasites to treat. These parasites can be killed by dipping affected fishes in saturated salt solutions.

TETRAHYMENA ("GUPPY KILLER")

Waters rich in organic nutrients favor the proliferation of a wide variety of ciliated protozoans. Although low numbers of these organisms are not considered harmful, large numbers can become a problem, especially if the fish are weakened and predisposed to acquiring disease. *Tetrahymena* infections are associated with nutrient-rich waters, so avoid overfeeding and keep the tank free of excessive debris and feces. Should an infection occur, water changes and the same therapeutic treatments used for ich should bring about a cure.

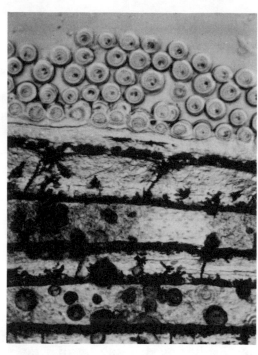

1. Fins of a fish with not one, but two types of parasitic ciliates; *Trichodina* on the surface and *Ichthyopthirius* encysted in the tissues. 2. An isolated *Trichodina* with its adhesive disc. Photos by Dr. Lom.

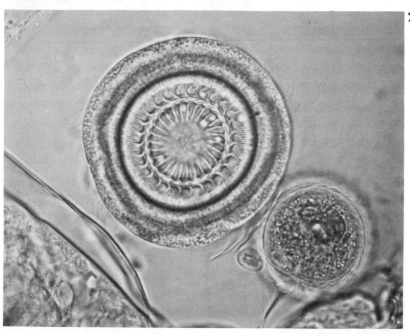

HEXAMITIASIS (HOLE-IN-THE-HEAD DISEASE)

Hexamitiasis is an infectious disease of fishes caused by the flagellated protozoan *Hexamita*. These parasites are rather pear-shaped with two nuclei and eight flagella (six anterior and two posterior). Although usually intestinal parasites capable of causing enteritis, these parasites can penetrate the intestinal wall and become distributed throughout the various body fluids and organs. Angelfish are considered to be quite resistant to infection of the internal organs, although they frequently harbor the parasite in the intestine. African cichlids and the discus are considered the most susceptible. In these species holes and tubular eruptions may develop in the skin, particularly in the region of the head. These holes in the head of discus have given rise to the very descriptive terminology "hole-in-the-head" disease. Other signs of disease include the excretion of white thread-like feces which adhere to the fish's vent and a general uninterest in feeding. As the disease progresses, affected fishes become emaciated as evidenced by a tucked-in abdomen.

A diagnosis is based upon identification of the protozoan in various organs of deceased fish or by examining freshly discharged feces of living fish. This procedure requires the use of a microscope. Generally, however, the aquarist can safely diagnose the condition based upon the appearance of typical lesions on the fish's head.

Metronidazole (Flagyl) is a prescription drug used to control trichomonad infections in man. It is also the drug of choice for treating hexamitiasis. Both external and internal applications of the drug will bring about a lasting cure. Flagyl baths should be given to fish showing external lesions at the rate of 250 mg./5 gallons of tank water. These 250 mg. pills should be crushed before placing them in the aquarium. Repeat the dosage every other day for a total of three treatments. While giving external treatments with the drug, the fish should also be receiving Flagyl-medicated food. The dosage rate is 1% medicated food for a duration of five days. If you have no means to measure out the drug or food, place a few finely pulverized granules of Flagyl in a small piece of meat and roll up the meat "enchilada style."

MICROSPORIDIAN DISEASE

Just as there are still many human diseases which cannot be successfully treated, there are a variety of incurable fish diseases. Some of these diseases remain sub-clinical and infected fishes can lead a relatively normal life, while others can be very severe and often fatal. One group of protozoan parasites, the microsporidians, are relatively common among freshwater tropical fishes. They have also been found infecting invertebrates, reptiles, amphibians and birds.

Most aquarists have probably heard of the so-called "neon tetra disease"; this is a microsporidian disease caused by the obligate intracellular parasite *Plistophora hyphessobryconis*. This parasite can actually dissolve away areas of muscle, not only in tetras but in many other fishes as well. Characins affected with this disease develop whitish areas which shine through the skin. Later in the course of the disease there is a complete discoloration of the normal skin pigmentation. Other signs of this disease include spinal curvature, equilibrium dysfunction, loss of weight, muscular paralysis, bizarre swimming behavior and fin degeneration. Some of the above signs of disease can also occur in other chronic diseases such as piscine tuberculosis, so care must be taken to avoid a misdiagnosis.

Another common group of microsporidians are in the genus *Nosema*. Various species have caused extensive damage to abdominal organs, viscera, musculature, gills and even the brains of tropical fishes. The clinical signs of disease vary depending on the particular tissues under attack. If death occurs, and it often does, it is either a result of organ dysfunction or a result of secondary bacterial or fungal invasions.

Because infected fishes serve as a reservoir of infection to other fishes, they should be removed from the exhibition aquarium. It then becomes a judgment decision whether these diseased fishes should be destroyed or given a chance to recover. Mildly infected aquarium fishes may survive some of the microsporidian diseases without apparent discomfort, while other diseases must certainly be excruciatingly painful. If affected fishes appear heavily infected and are suffering, they should be destroyed. Do not flush the dead fishes down the toilet or grind them in a garbage disposal—this could lead to contamination of natural waterways. Infected fishes should be either burned or buried away from water drainages.

Because there is no cure for any of these microsporidian diseases, about the best an aquarist can do is to be able to recognize them for what they are and take steps to prevent other fishes from contracting the disease. Should an epizootic occur in your aquarium, completely disinfect the tank before restocking it with healthy fishes. Signs of the developing disease may not be present at the time of purchase and quarantine, thus the introduction of microsporidian infected fishes is a definite possibility. You can reduce the likelihood of microsporidian problems by providing your fishes with optimal living conditions and being careful not to feed them infected tissues of fishes.

WORM DISEASE
Flukes

The trematodes or flukes are flattened, non-segmented parasites which are covered with cuticle. Flukes have external hooks and suckers which enable them to attach to the host. According to whether their development is direct or indirect, the flukes are broadly divided into monogenetic and digenetic trematodes. Monogenetic flukes do not require an intermediate host, while an intermediate host such as a snail is required for the life cycle of the digenetic flukes.

The most common fluke parasites of aquarium fishes are the monogenetic variety. They are external parasites of the skin, fins and gills.

GYRODACTYLUS

Most gyrodactylids live on the skin and fins of fishes, where they feed on epithelial cells and tissue fluids. Occasionally they are found infecting the gills. The most common signs of disease include a whitish discoloration of the skin, emaciation and fraying of the fins. If the fins are heavily parasitized, the soft inter-ray tissues can be destroyed so that only the harder fin rays remain. The eyes may also become opaque and eventually the fish may become blind. Heavy infestations cause small wounds which permit the entry of bacterial and fungal invaders. These flukes are just barely visible with the unaided eye. Unlike *Dactylogyrus*, the gyrodactylids lack visible eye spots. They are hermaphroditic and bear their offspring live, one at a time. The young are born fully developed and capable of immediate parasitization. These flukes are easily controlled with short duration formalin baths (30 drops of formaldehyde per gallon of water). These short baths (up to 30 minutes maximum) can be repeated in a few days if a reinfestation should occur. Some of the other agents which have been effectively used to kill these flukes include trichlorfon (Masoten), copper sulfate, malachite green, methylene blue, potassium permanganate and sodium chloride.

DACTYLOGYRUS

Another common monogenetic fluke is *Dactylogyrus*. Four black eyes are clearly visible at the anterior extremity of this fluke. Unlike *Gyrodactylus*, this genus is oviparous and the adults die after shedding large numbers of eggs. These flukes destroy much of the gill tissue, which can cause signs of respiratory distress. The gill cover may become somewhat distended as the edges of the gill lamellae become thickened. Areas of gill destruction may become grayish white in color. The treatment of dactylogyrid infections is the same as for gyrodactylid infestations.

Roundworms

The nematodes or roundworms are unsegmented worms which have a cylindrical and elongate body. They differ from the flukes and tapeworms by possession of a complete digestive tract and (with few exceptions) separate sexes. The life-cycle may be direct or include an intermediate host. Among the roundworms which parasitize fishes, an invertebrate such as a copepod is always involved as the first intermediate host.

CAMALLANUS

One of the most common nematode parasites of tropical fishes is *Camallanus*. These semitransparent to blood-red worms are small (¼ to ½ inches long) but deadly. Their red coloration is derived from the fish blood which they ingest. These parasites cause anemia, poor growth, eventual emaciation and often death among small livebearers. Guppies, mollies, platies and swordtails seem to be especially prone to acquiring a *Camallanus* infection. Fishes become infected in outdoor production ponds when they ingest infective copepods, the intermediate host. Also, fishes can become infected if copepods are fed in aquariums. Whenever live foods (such as *Daphnia*) are harvested from natural waters you run the risk of introducing infective intermediate hosts such as *Camallanus*-laden copepods. A diagnosis of *Camallanus* infection is relatively simple as these parasites have an affinity for protruding from the

1. An African cichlid *(Haplochromis polystigma)* from Lake Malawi with wounds caused by an *Oodinium*-like parasite. Photo by Dr. H.-H. Reichenbach-Klinke. 2. *Oodinoides vastator* cells proliferating in the gills of a fish. 3. Note the many cilia around the cells of *I. multifiliis* during the infective, or swarmer, stage. Photo by Dr. H.-H. Reichenbach-Klinke. 4. A mature cell of *I. multifiliis.* Frickhinger photo. 5. A platy *(Xiphophorus maculatus)* with *Ichthyophthirius multifiliis* infection on the fins. Photo by M.F. Roberts.

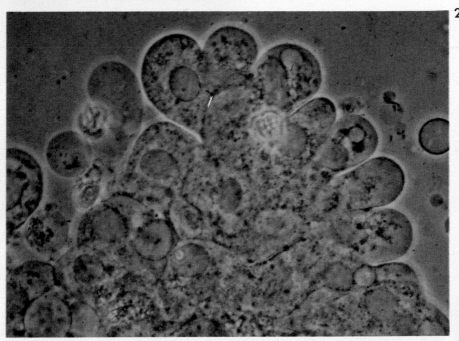

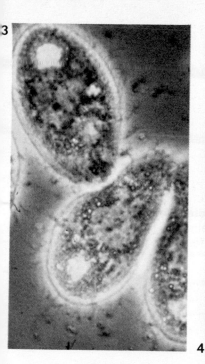

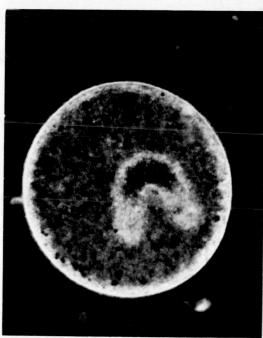

fish's vent. When startled, the parasites retreat into the safety of the fish's rectum. Piperazine, a dewormer for kittens and puppies, is the dewormer of choice. You can obtain piperazine tablets from your local veterinarian. They should be pulvarized and mixed with a prepared gelatinous food mixture at the rate of 25 mg./10 grams of food.

Feed this medicated food daily for up to a maximum of 10 days.

Tapeworms

Tapeworms (cestodes) are flattened worms which may or may not show obvious segmentation in the adult stage. Generally their head (scolex) bears suckers and may also have attachment hooks. No digestive tract is present, and the adults are hermaphroditic with the male and female organs being present in each segment or proglottid. All of the tapeworms are internal parasites. The adults parasitize the intestinal tract of a wide variety of animals, while the larvae (plerocercoids) infect a variety of body organs and tissues. Fishes can act as either intermediate hosts and contain plerocercoid cysts or as final hosts and contain adult tapeworms in their intestine. While damage occurs as a result of adult cestode parasitism, the real damage results when the larvae invade the fish's tissues and vital body organs. There is no treatment for the plerocercoids, which can cause cystic lesions and even death. Adult tapeworms can be effectively removed from the fish's intestinal tract with the use of niclosamide (Yomesan) at the rate of 50 mg./10 grams of food. A single feeding of Yomesan-impregnated food should be sufficient to kill the adult cestode parasites.

PARASITIC CRUSTACEANS

Crustaceans were evolving long before the appearance of the first fish, so initially there were no fish parasites in this group. When fish began evolving some 400 million years ago, so did some free-living crustaceans. Competition for food was apparently keen million of years ago because some copepods (and isopods too) left their former ecological niche and adapted themselves to become fish parasites. By developing specialized structures for attachment and feeding, these parasitic copepods parted ways with their free-living ancestors and became successfully adapted parasites. In even the earliest descriptions of fish, there were mentions of parasitic crustaceans. Because of this long and successful heritage, we know these animals are both specialized and adaptable. Parasitic adaptability is an important phenomenon, especially when we concern ourselves with trying to destroy these parasites.

Parasitic relationships imply a harmful association where the parasite lives at the expense of the host. In this sense, every parasite living in or on a fish exerts some degree of harmful influence on its host. Harm from parasitic copepods is attributable to mechanical damage, depriving the host of nutrients, secreting toxic substances and rendering the fish more susceptible to secondary infections. Parasitic copepods can kill their host by any one of the above factors, but usually a combination of these harmful influences is what results in the demise of the fish.

Just how common are these parasitic copepods? Unfortunately they are all too common, both in the natural environment and in captivity. Some of the more common parasitic copepods include the fish "lice" (*Argulus*), the anchor "worm" (*Lernaea*) and the gill parasite *Ergasilus*.

ARGULUS

The species of *Argulus* native to American waters are not sufficiently adaptable to become a problem in tropical aquariums, but warm water tropical species can be imported along with the fishes and become a nuisance. If you have a koi or goldfish pond, be cautious when you transport material from natural waterways to your established pond—you may also be transporting *Argulus*!

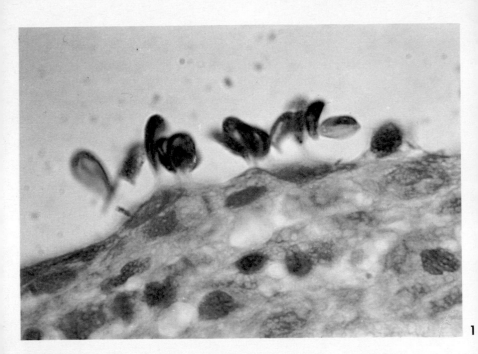

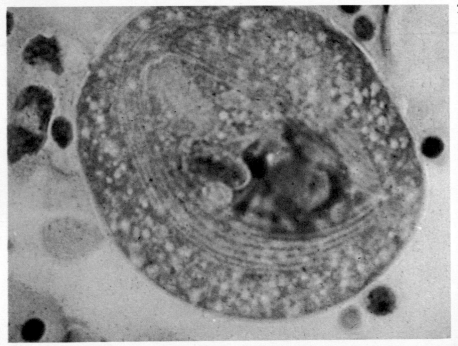

70

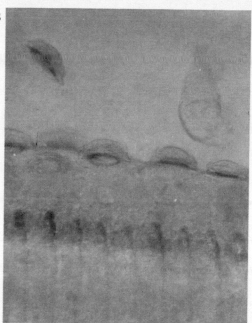

1. A swarm of *Costia necatrix* cells on the skin of a brown trout. 2. A very much enlarged photograph of *Chilodinella cyprini*. Photo by Dr. H.-H. Reichenbach-Klinke. 3. The gill surface of a catfish with some cells of *Trichodina*. Photo by Dr. Fred Meyer. 4. Under high magnification and proper lighting it is possible to recognize the cilia of *Trichodina*. Frickhinger photo.

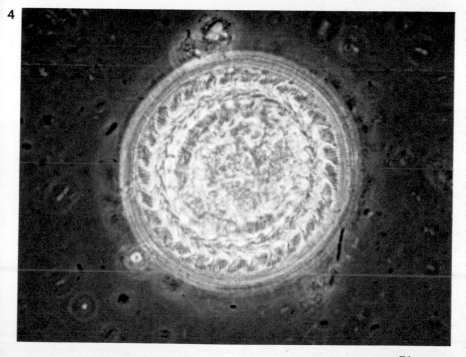

71

Because the diameter of *Argulus's* needle-like stylet is smaller than that of the fish's red blood cells, whole blood presumably is not ingested. Toxic substances released from the proboscis glands of *Argulus* may help this parasite obtain its lunch, but this fluid certainly has an adverse effect on the fish. Localized reddening, and swelling of the tissue and the death of young fishes have been blamed on this potent toxin.

If the parasites are too numerous to remove by hand, baths in the contact insecticide trichlorfon will effectively destroy the parasite. Trichlorfon is sold at both plant supply stores and livestock outlets under a variety of trade names such as Dipterex, Dylox, Dyrex, Chlorphos, Bot-X, Masoten and Neguvon. The concentration of the active ingredient varies with the different products. Based upon the level of active ingredients, the therapeutic dosage is 0.25 to 1.0 ppm. The drug is rapidly hydrolyzed and becomes inactive within a few hours after being placed in warm water aquariums. In therapeutic dosages trichlorfon has no adverse effect on the beneficial bacterial flora in the biofilter. If necessary, the treatment can be repeated once weekly for up to three weeks. As is the case with all poisonous substances, extreme caution should be used when handling and storing to avoid accidental poisoning of children or pets.

ANCHOR "WORM" (*LERNAEA*)

The lernaeids have become so extensively modified in the adult form that they do not even look like their free-living ancestors. They are more worm-like in appearance, hence the common name "anchor worm." *Lernaea* infestations affect a wide variety of freshwater fishes in moderately warm waters. It is not unusual for aquarium fishes to be parasitized by *Lernaea,* but only the female "worms" are parasitic. Their "anchor" becomes embedded in the gill or skin tissues of the host while she saps the host of nourishment.

Two egg sacs are typically attached to her posterior end.

Depending upon the number of parasites, sites of attachment and size of the host, lernaeids can produce only minor damage or they can cause the death of your fish.

Salt solutions have been suggested as a method of killing newly emerged larvae (nauplii), but this treatment has no effect on the adults. Potassium permanganate (0.1% solution) can be painted on the exposed parts of the lernaeid, being careful to avoid contact with the skin. After the parasite dies, it can be removed with tweezers. Trichlorfon (Dylox, Masoten) is perhaps the most effective way to destroy lernaeid parasites. The same treatment regimen which was used to eradicate *Argulus* works well against lernaeids; use 0.25 to 1.0 ppm of active ingredient placed in the aquarium once weekly for up to three successive weeks. This therapy will kill the copepods, but the "head" of the parasite often remains embedded, thereby leaving an unsightly scar.

ERGASILUS

Ergasilus is a genus of parasitic copepods which feed mainly on the gill cells of a wide variety of freshwater fishes including tropical aquarium fishes. It is primarily the females which are parasitic upon fishes; the males are mainly free-swimmers which die shortly after copulation. These parasitic copepods feed upon the cells of the gill epithelium by means of extra-cellular digestion. They can severely damage the gills and even cause hemorrhaging of the gill vessels. Heavily affected fishes generally show evidence of respiratory distress such as gasping at the surface, scratching the opercles on aquarium objects and breathing rapidly. When material from the gills is examined microscopically, these parasites can be recognized by their pronounced clasper-like claws. The treatment for ergasilosis is the same as for *Argulus* and *Lernaea*—baths in the insecticide trichlorfon.

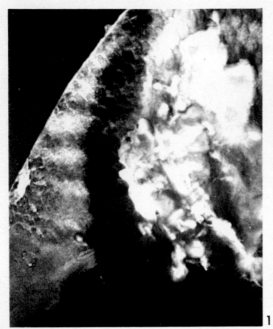
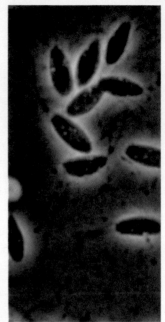

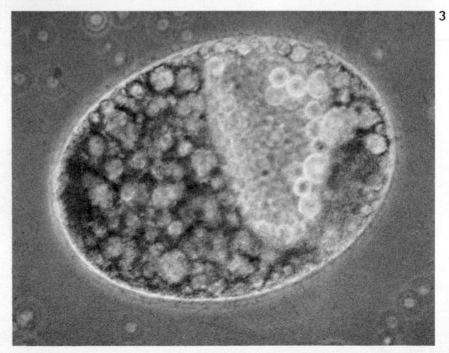

4

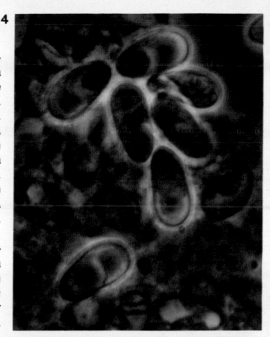

1. A discus fish *(Symphysodon discus)* with a festering wound on the head caused by Hexamita. Photo by Dr. H.-H. Reichenbach-Klinke. 2. A swarm of *Hexamita* taken from the intestines of a fish. A Frickhinger photo. 3. An enlarged photograph of *Tetrahymena*. A Frickhinger photo. 4. Spores of *Plistophora*. Photo by Dr. R. Summerfelt. 5. A neon tetra *(Paracheirodon innesi)* with symptoms of *Plistophora* infection. A Frickhinger photo.

5

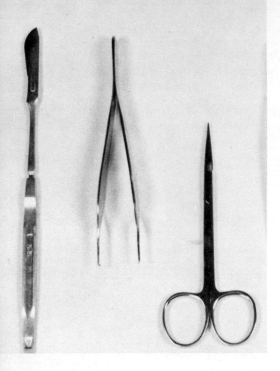

A few basic tools needed for a post-mortem examination of a fish: scalpel, scissors, and tweezers. *Below:* The gill of a fish in the process of being removed after the gill arch (bony part) has been cut. Gills must be examined, because it is a common site of attachment for external parasites. Photos by Dr. Mark Dulin.

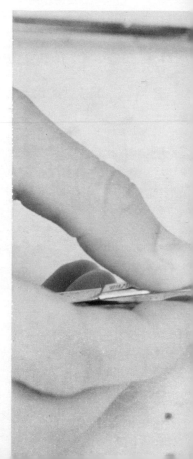

Post-Mortem Examination

If you are an inquisitive aquarist and are conscientious about your fishes' health, then undoubtedly you want to know why a particular fish died. By knowing the specific cause of death, steps can often be taken to prevent future mortalities. For your fish's sake, it is best to diagnose a particular disease based upon the clinical signs of disease which may appear during life. For example, the appearance of white spots on your fish's skin gives a clue that it may be suffering from "ich." Sometimes these useful signs are missing and the fish dies for no apparent reason. It is especially these deaths from mysterious maladies which should be thoroughly investigated.

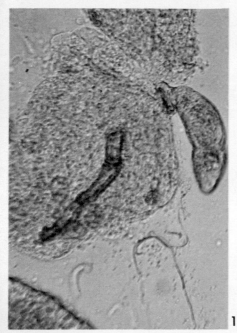

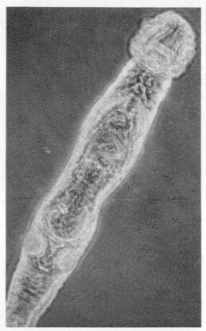

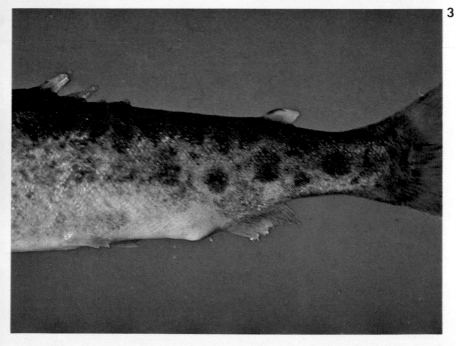

4

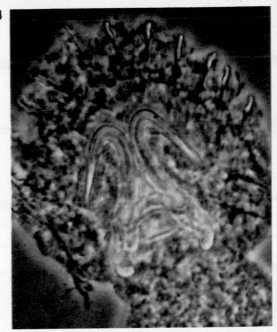

1, *Gyrodactylus* sp. feeding on the cells of the skin of a fish. 2. *Gyrodactylus elegans* with developing young in its body cavity. Frickhinger photo. 3. The fins of this fish have been destroyed by the feeding activity of *Gyrodactylus*. 4. Close-up of the holdfast structure of *Gyrodactylus:* two large principal hooks and a series of smaller hooks. Photo by Dr. H.-H. Reichenbach-Klinke. 5. A gill filament of a fish with heavy infestation of *Dactylogyrus.* Photo by Dr. W. Rogers.

5

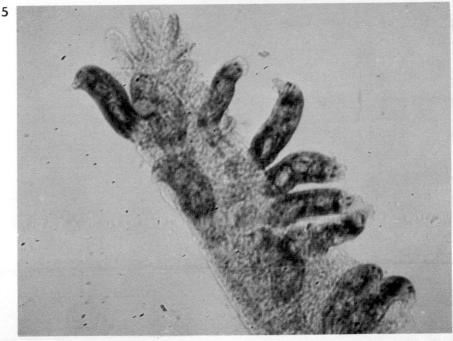

Many of the techniques of investigation are too sophisticated and complex to be performed by the average aquarist, but the basic post-mortem examination is relatively simple. Of course a diagnosis cannot always be made based upon the simplified scheme of examination which follows. It takes a good deal of training and experience (and sometimes luck) to successfully diagnose fish diseases. The most fundamental prerequisite is a thorough understanding of fish anatomy. Before you can recognize abnormal tissue, you must first be familiar with the normal. Many times the aquarist will still need to obtain professional help—you certainly won't be very proficient on your first dissection, but everyone has to start somewhere.

Now I know some of you are a bit squeamish and could never dissect your deceased pet. Admittedly, this subject may appeal only to those aquarists who are biologically inclined. I also want to emphasize that there are certain inherent dangers involved in conducting a post-mortem examination (necropsy). Aside from the possibility of cutting yourself with a scalpel, an aquarist could become infected with certain bacteria known to exist in diseased fish. For example, fish-packers in sardine canneries sometimes acquire lesions on the hands caused by bacteria of the genus *Serratia*. More rarely, aquarists have acquired localized skin lesions from handling fishes suffering from piscine tuberculosis (mycobacteriosis). I am not trying to scare you, just warn you! The chances of your acquiring an infection from handling a diseased fish are certainly minimal, but caution should be exercised just the same. Just as you wouldn't swim in a lake if you had cuts and scratches on your body, you shouldn't dissect fish if you have a cut finger. As an additional precaution, rubber gloves could be worn by the investigator.

Only a few instruments are needed for a standard necropsy procedure. If a scalpel, iris scissors and fine-pointed thumb forceps are not readily available, a single-edged

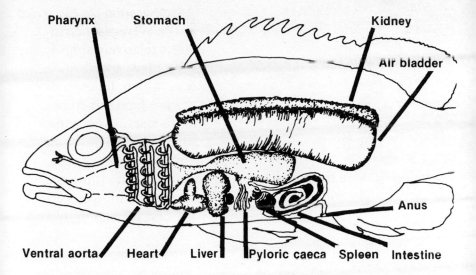

Pharynx Stomach Kidney Air bladder

Anus

Ventral aorta Heart Liver Pyloric caeca Spleen Intestine

Diagrammatic illustration of the internal anatomy of a fish. Only the major organs are shown.

Samples of the body fluids of a fish can be taken with the aid of an ordinary syringe. Photo by Dr. M. Dulin.

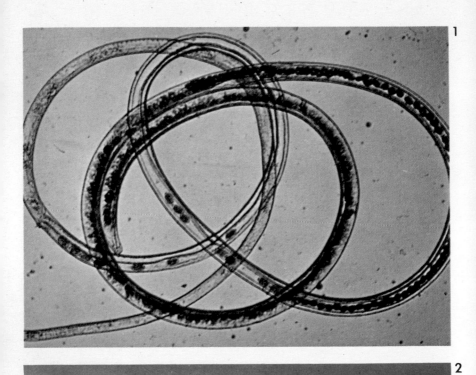

1. Hairworms are roundworms often present in the digestive tract of freshwater fishes. Their larval stages occur in small crustaceans. Photo by Dr. H.-H. Reichenbach-Klinke. 2. Adult tapeworms (cestodes) in the gut of a channel catfish. Photo by Dr. W. Rogers. 3. Plerocercoid (larval stage) of cestode on the surface of the liver of a trout. Photo by Dr. R. Texter. 4. Four distinct suckers are present in the scolex or head of a cestode. Photo by K.E. Sneed.

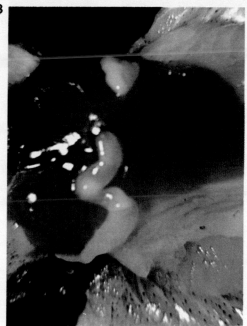

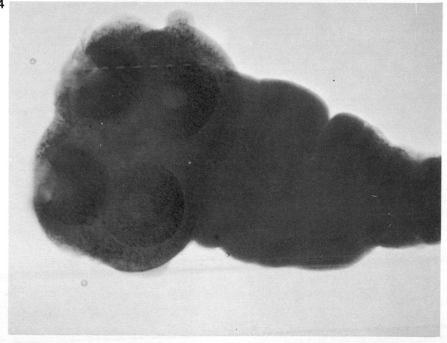

razor blade, manicure scissors and household tweezers will suffice. If you have access to a microscope, by all means use it to your advantage. If not, an ordinary magnifying lens will help you detect parasites and lesions. A good camera with close-up capabilities is a valuable asset; it can be used to photograph any unusual pathological changes. Should you need to obtain help in diagnosing the disease, color transparencies (slides) accompanied by preserved and frozen tissues will aid the fish pathologist in diagnosing the disease. Tissues submitted for histopathologic examination should be placed in either 10% buffered neutral formalin or Bouin's fixative. Tissues submitted for bacterial isolation should either be refrigerated or frozen.

Only recent mortalities are valuable for a necropsy procedure. Tropical fishes will rapidly undergo decomposition in a warm tank, and these post-mortem changes can interfere with a proper diagnosis. If you cannot examine the dead fish immediately, refrigerate it until later. Generally it is best to necropsy the fish upon discovery; bagging it in the refrigerator only leads to procrastination and will delay your knowing the cause of death. Other fish may soon show clinical signs of the same disease, and unless you know why a given fish died, you are not likely to know how to treat your surviving fish.

EXTERNAL EXAMINATION
SKIN

Examine the skin for external parasites or lesions such as raised scales, nodules, ulcers, nipping wounds or reddened areas. If you have a microscope, make a skin scraping from the periphery of lesions, from beneath raised scales, behind the fins or from any "suspicious" area on the fish. This material can be placed on a microscope slide along with a drop of water, cover-slipped and examined microscopically.

FINS

Careful examination of the fins is important because

1. Eye of a fish with encysted flukes that are visible through the pupil. 2. The prominent structure on the dorsal side of the body cavity of this dissected piranha is the gas or swim bladder. Photo by Dr. H.R. Axelrod.

2

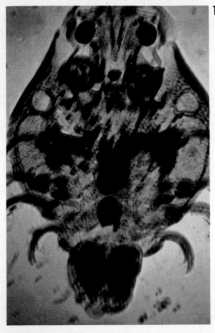

1. *Argulus* is commonly called fish louse. Photo by Dr. E. Elkan.
2. *Argulus* attached on the belly of fish. Photo by Dr. P. Ghittino.
3. An unidentified parasitic copepod attached to the gills of a trout. Photo by Dr. M.P. Dulin.
4. Early larval stage or nauplius stage of *Lernaea*. Dr. F. Meyer.
5. Part of *Lernaea* which is modified for anchoring to the host. Frickhinger photo.

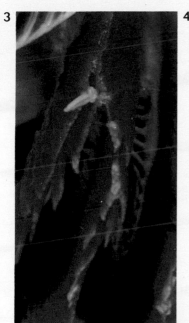

3

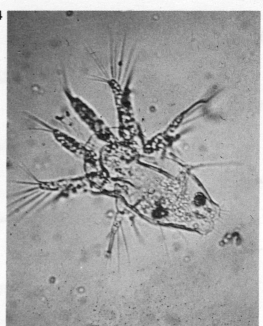

4

5

many diseases cause a loss of tissue integrity. Frayed fins and reddening at the base of fins should be noted, as they are often a sign of an acute systemic bacterial infection. Frayed fins without reddening may indicate attacks from more aggressive fishes, malnutrition or a variety of external parasites. Examine material scraped from frayed fins for microscopic organisms.

BODY OPENINGS
Carefully inspect the mouth for reddening or ulceration. Check the vent; a swollen or reddened vent area may indicate a gastrointestinal problem.

GENERAL MORPHOLOGY
Examine the fish from the side as well as from above. Deformations in normal body symmetry should be noted. Is one eye protruding (popeye) or the abdomen swollen (dropsy)? Record your findings.

GILLS
The gills should be red during life and shortly after death. Pale gills generally mean the fish is anemic. Look closely at the gill filaments. Parasites may be attached to the filaments and cause a ragged appearance. If you have a microscope, remove a gill arch and then snip a small section of filaments from the arch. Place this on a microscope slide with a drop of water and apply a cover-slip. Examine microscopically under low power and low illumination. If a microscope is not available, look at the gills with a magnifying lens.

INTERNAL EXAMINATION
THE DISSECTION
Using a sharp scalpel or single-edged razor blade, make a very small incision just below the heart. Insert one blade of the scissors into this opening and lift up on the skin. Cut

posteriorly along the ventral midline, lifting up with the buried scissor blade as you cut. This will reduce the chances of your puncturing the gastrointestinal tract. When your incision reaches the vent area, cut upward on the fish's left side. Continue this incision cranially all the way to the gills so that you have essentially removed the left body wall of the fish.

PERITONEAL CAVITY

Look at the abdominal wall and musculature for reddened areas or nodules. Check for fluid accumulation within the abdominal cavity (ascites), an indication of "dropsy." Observe all the visible body organs closely before you start moving tissues around with a probe. If you see any obvious abnormalities you may want to photograph them or at least record them in your notebook.

VISCERA EXAMINATION

Examine the entire gastrointestinal (G.I.) tract from the esophagus to the vent. Note whether there is food in the gut or whether the intestinal tract feels flaccid and fluid-filled. Snip the esophagus and pull the G.I. tract posteriorly along with the attached liver, spleen, pancreas and pyloric cecae. Cut the vent free of its muscular attachment and set the viscera on a moist towel for later examination.

HEART

Snip the heart free and look for lesions and areas of discoloration. Now is a good time to observe the blood of recent mortalities. The blood should be red, not chocolate brown. Brown blood indicates the fish was suffering from nitrite toxicity caused by a buildup of metabolic wastes.

GONADS

The gonads (sexual organs) are often hard to find, especially if the fish is not sexually mature. If you notice

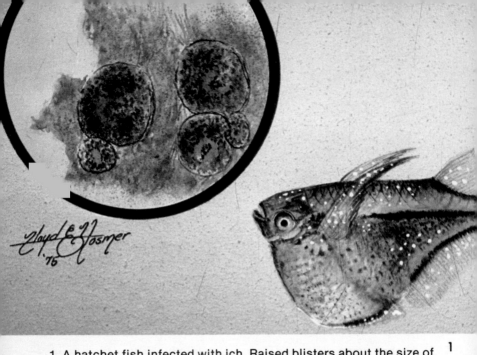

1. A hatchet fish infected with ich. Raised blisters about the size of a grain of salt are present on the fins and body. 2. A blue gourami with gill flukes. Flukes damage the gill tissues and cause respiratory difficulties. Illustrations © 1979 by Wardley Products Co., Inc.

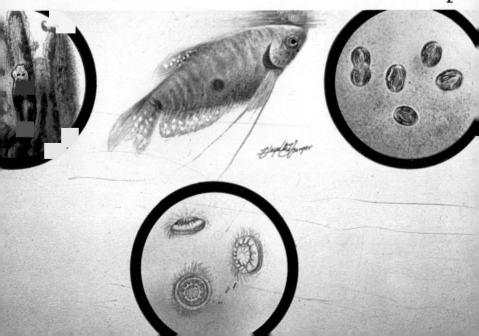

1

2

1 1. Anchor worm (left) and fish louse (right) can be present in goldfish, causing sores in areas of attachment on the fish. 2. Fungus is suspected whenever white filamentous or cotton-like material is present on any part of the body of a fish, such as an **2** angelfish. Illustration © 1979 by Wardley Products Co., Inc.

them lying across the air bladder, make a note of the sex. The ovaries appear egg-filled, while the testes are white and exude milt if the male is "ripe."

AIR (SWIM) BLADDER

Examine the air bladder, then remove it to expose the kidney.

KIDNEY

Check the kidney for obvious swelling, then remove the sheath which covers the kidney. Check for abscesses or other lesions. Examine the ureters and urinary bladder for evidence of parasitism.

LIVER AND GALL BLADDER

Now go back to the viscera you had previously removed and examine the liver and gall bladder for any pathological changes. If swelling and lesions are present, record these findings.

The gall bladder may be very swollen with greenish bile if the fish has not eaten recently. Parasites may be lodged in the bile duct, so examine thoroughly.

SPLEEN

Examine the spleen for evidence of lesions or swelling. It should have discrete edges and not be rounded or have a football appearance.

INTERNAL G.I. TRACT EXAM

Run the intestine between your fingers and feel for nodules in the intestinal wall. Fibrotic nodules are often the site of thorny-headed worm attachment. Open the entire gut from the esophagus to the rectum and look for the presence of food, lesions or parasites. If you find parasites you may want to preserve them for later identification (rubbing alcohol or vodka will suffice). Check for microscopic parasites by making a wet-mount preparation from material scraped from the rectal wall. Add a drop of water to this material before applying a coverslip so that motile organisms can be provided with a medium for movement. You may see *Hexamita* swimming about; these flagellated protozoans can cause enteritis and hole-in-the-head disease of discus and other cichlids.

BRAIN

Using your scalpel or razor blade, cut off a portion of the cranium. Do this cautiously and don't use the scalpel as a "pick" because a piece of the blade may break off and fly in your face. Use forceps or tweezers to chip off the cranium. Check the brain for lesions and reddened areas. Systemic bacterial diseases can often invade the brain, causing a reddened (meningitis) condition.

If you just cannot force yourself to dissect your pet or simply lack the skill to interpret what you find, there are commercial laboratories that perform post-mortems for a small fee. The addresses of the laboratories, their charges and requirements are given in occasional lists in *Tropical Fish Hobbyist* magazine.